Key Account Hack

8 steps to creating massive and predictable growth from your key clients in 90 days

By: Jermaine Edwards

Acknowledgement

There isn't a day that goes by where I'm not thankful for my family. The first thank you goes to my ever patient and understanding wife Heather and kids Sean, Kaya, Indiana and Emelia who make life worthwhile and awesome. To my mum Margurita and dad Norman and my brothers Andre, Devann and Omar who inspire me as they pursue their dreams.

When starting my journey of writing this book I was working for a great global training company and a book seemed far away. The team at Speak First have been a huge influence on my personal growth. The awesome team I worked with were Jun Man, Matthew Sherman, Oscar Famakinwa, Sophie Atkinson, Van Sharma, Terri Coyle, Georgia Potter, Stuart Robinson, Helen Blythe, Jack Bavister and Steve Bavister. Special thanks to Amanda Vickers who has seen me at the earliest part of my career until now and is a great role model.

The great support of Fizzle and the mastermind team that keeps me accountable and focused on the vision of impacting a million sales professionals around the world. Heena Modi, Chris Thatcher and Ragu Ramdas.

To all those who gave up their time for me to interview them. Christina Bowe, James Worford, Siddartha, Jan Lind, Paul Newsome, Donald Kelly, DB International and so many more.

If there is one phrase that has kept me focused on the goal it's that the *'greatest contribution you can give to the world is an investment in yourself so that others benefit from the returns'*.

This book is only the beginning.

Contents

Introduction

If you're reading these words then, like me, you're ready for a change. You're ready for a different kind of success in your business, sales and client relationships. Five years ago I was the same. Like other key account professionals I was tired of all the technical jargon out there, telling you to fill in sheets, stats and forms that led to arbitrary customer data. Data that never really helps you to understand the fundamentals of how you can help your customers buy, retain them and grow your customers in a significant way.

Or perhaps like me you just didn't know where to go next! How do you deepen client relationships and see larger sales than ever? This book was written to help move you from that unknown into clarity. You can take daily steps to see even greater customer success.

If you commit to reading, applying and reviewing what is in this book it will

- Show you how to deepen your client relationships,
- Help you grow your key customer sales by 30% in the next 90 days,
- Help you develop new and positive habits with a more fluid way of viewing your customer accounts,
- Help you to pivot in more challenging times and, more importantly, continue making above average progress that many account managers will not see in your market.

At the end of this book you will

- Know the approaches in your sales process you need to change to have more profitable customer conversations.

○ Understand the key strategies and tactics you can use to deepen trust and build more effective relationships.
○ Know how to implement a sequence of engagements for predictable and explosive sales from existing customers.
○ Know how to connect, engage and deepen your influence with multiple key stakeholders.

This will all be grounded in approaches, strategies and tactics that work for you in the real world you sell in.

This book is primarily for account managers and key account managers. But you can easily use a number of the approaches and tools if you're a freelancer or solopreneur, a sales manager getting your team focused on the right client priorities or a small business owner wanting more direction on how to serve and grow your clients. It's for all those who know they can do more with their clients so that everybody wins.

What to expect

Let's be real. You're an experienced professional and some of what you'll read you will know. Some of these skills you may do well already. When you are confronted with a skill in this book my hope is that you will ask yourself these three questions:

● How well do I do this?
● How do I know?
● Do I get the consistent growth in sales with most of the clients I manage?

This book is here to challenge your current assumptions and increase the awareness of areas you could improve to give you more consistent success and greater results. You'll get access to the resources you need with guides and links to external resources at the back of this book.

Three things you need to be aware of

Key account management is all about three areas of engagement with your customers: **relational, strategic and tactical**. It's very easy in key account or large account management to focus heavily on strategy. We can be so bombarded by academic research (SWOT analysis and strategic planning) that we miss a very important consideration. *To experience explosive sales and relationship results from your key clients you need to focus just as much on relational and tactical engagement as the strategic.*

They're all just as important as the other. The strategic engagement helps you to know where you're going. But, the relational and tactical engagement is what actually drives the sale forward. No one has really tackled the implications of this in practice.

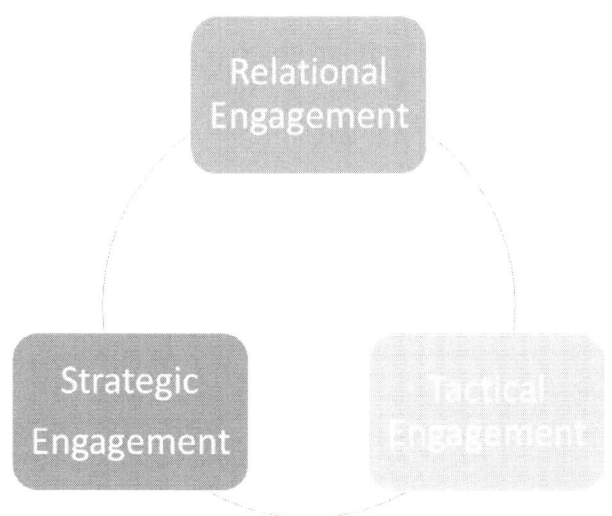

Relational Engagement

Your ability to connect with your clients and deepen trust and influence.

Many miss this in account management. We're told we need to build relationships, which is critical to customer success. But what does that actually look like? How will you know things are working? What will you use to build those connections, amplify trust and deepen those relationships most important to you? This is what relational engagement is all about. You need to consider what you want your client relationship to look like and how you get there. Without a focus on this you limit your ability to grow your influence and opportunities.

Strategic Engagement

Your ability to align yours and your customer's goals to one or multiple mutually beneficial outcomes.

You and your managers can spend a lot of time on strategic tasks that, while helpful, don't necessarily move sales forward. Strategic engagement is also where you'll set expectations with your client on how you'll work best together. This includes your business growth goals. It may also include what I call *power connections*. These are connections with key influencers or stakeholders that move your strategy forward. Strategic engagement ultimately helps give you clarity on where to go and where the potential opportunities are for present and future success with your customer.

Tactical Engagement

Your ability to deliver on the right things to win consistently.

This area probably gets the least amount of time and thought dedicated to it in key account management. What are the daily and weekly tactical implications for every strategy or plan set with your client and internally within your business? This could include how you decide to build relationships, how you align the rest of your internal departments to support customer success or how you execute growth promises with your board and account management team. If not considered carefully and if you lack a clear process for how you execute on strategy, *you may still have wins but you'll have very few business transforming client successes.*

This book is not about key account management strategy. This book focuses on the tactical and relational engagement you need for customer success, because, they drive the movement of the sale.

The question is, "How do you apply this?", considering you'll have your own client goals, customer history and personal targets.

I've created an 8 step system of thinking that fits into any sales process or stage you are in with your client conversations. You'll notice in this system I've highlighted what I call the 4 pillars for customer growth success in key account management. These skills and qualities need to be consistent throughout your selling relationship to continue amplifying the success you already have.

Those 4 pillars are the ability to
- Amplify Trust
- Reduce Risk
- Make Power Connections
- Create Value that Matters

All this and more will be explained as you go step-by-step through the book. At the end you will have a clear, replicable and predictable path to more profitable customer conversations. You may also want to go immediately to the resource section for the link address to all the free resources available to help support you through this book. So let's get started!

Step 1

CLARITY THROUGH EXPECTATIONS

Expectation is the killer of most organisations' customer growth because they never really understand what their customer wants.

Does this statement ring true in your mind? Aren't customers indecisive and unsure? Do they even know what they want? The truth is our customers are more informed than ever, but their expectations can and will change based on where they are. They may not always have the clarity of what they want but they definitely know what they want to experience.

Taking a step back, at whatever stage you are in your client relationship to get clear on expectations is the most important step you can take. Without that clarity you're simply running on assumptions and momentary glimpses of 'I think so' and maybes. Here's the clarity of expectation I want you to go after: your expectations should be *an agreed practice, value or behavior of a person, or between multiple people, that defines how you approach particular tasks, circumstances and decisions.*

If you begin your client conversations with this definition you can approach your client with the right messaging and with more clarity and confidence. This must be an agreement that is shared and committed to by you and your customer. With this in place no matter what changes may come you'll have a foundation to work from. There are two sides to expectation that you need to be aware of. There is the expectation of practice between you and your customer and the expectation of importance.

The expectation of practice is what you're contracted to do. The expectation of importance is the honest reality that for many of your customers, you may not be a key provider. Why should they commit the time, resources and the levels of access you're asking for?

Guess what? Your customer behavior will change as their needs and industry does. Just as your business has limited capacity to truly manage key accounts, your customers may have limited capacity to manage key providers and allow them to integrate fully within their business. Once a new person comes into the business, a key person leaves, or re-organisation happens you might be in trouble. We've all experienced those sales altering disruptions!

It's this idea of the expectation of importance that is not spoken about. In order to bring greater clarity to this critical area I've called it the

CLIENT EXPECTATION GAP. This is the distance between your perceived experience of who you are to your client and where your client perceives it is for them and their business. The further the distance between those two perceptions the more vulnerable your business is to churn and missed opportunity.

Exercise: Let's do a quick exercise to test this. Read the following statements and make a note of where you believe you and your company fit with your top spending client today.

1. You are a fully integrated provider into most areas and departments of your client's business and have a known, recognised and strategic partnership. Your product or service is seen as very important to their business needs.

2. You are an integrated provider in some areas of your client's business. You have a recognised partnership with some departments and your product or solution is seen as important to their business needs.

3. You are somewhat integrated in your client's business but are only known to specific people. Your product or service is seen as important.

4. You are not integrated into your client's business but do offer a product or service perceived as somewhat important to their business.

5. You are not integrated into your client's business. Your product or service is perceived as helpful but not integral.

6. What did you discover about where you think your business is? Was it what you expected? Is this what your client thinks?

Whatever the result you've discovered, it tells you something about what you might need to ask such as:

- ✓ What are your customer's expectations of you? (based on the above definition)
- ✓ How do they view your partnership?
- ✓ Is this aligned with your current perspective?

How you respond and engage with these questions matters for your long-term growth and sales success. With this clarity you can apply the right strategies and conversations to change or improve on what you're doing already and avoid the dreaded 'churn' and potentially missed sales opportunities.

Let's get practical and tactical. In order to get clarity in both levels of expectation of work and importance

1. You need to determine the current expectations your client has of you and how you work together. Start with how you work together today. Using the expectation definition to guide the questions you might ask.
2. Be honest about what the relationship looks like today. Don't be surprised if you're not the most important supplier to them. Just be the most memorable and you can go from there.
3. Be clear on what you want from the relationship and aim to align your sales process as close to your client's as possible. You need to have this in place to ensure you're meeting and delivering on expectations every time.
4. Document what you discuss. Share this with your client and everyone connected to your client in your business. The more transparent you are the clearer the responsibilities are to everyone involved. It also means there are fewer misunderstandings when working with your client. This gives you room to focus on all the right things rather than being distracted by everything.

SKILL UPLOAD

ONE ADDITIONAL SKILL THAT WILL AID HOW YOU PREPARE FOR GAINING CLARITY OF EXPECTATION

How to Ensure Your Questions Really Get You Answers That Matter

"Questions are the answer"— Allan Pearse

As simple as that phrase is, it should change your whole perspective on the value and benefit of great questions in sales. As a key account manager asking questions is a critical skill. It helps clients discover new solutions and challenges you to change behaviours that aren't effective.

The questions you ask in your customer conversations need to be challenged. The archetypal questions of who, where, what, how or closed and open questions are peppered throughout your trainings and education. These trainings are great for telling you what types of questions you *could* ask.

However, they give no guidance in knowing *how* you develop questions that get you answers that matter. We can be so caught up in asking questions that we never ask ourselves, "Do I know the reason why?" or "What's the purpose?" It's those answers that should shape the direction of your questions.

What is that one thing that you really want to know? Why? And does it help you and the other person achieve a goal? Of course there are a whole host of reasons you might need to ask questions to your clients and colleagues. All of these are helpful reasons to ask questions as you focus on expectations.

✓ To understand what specific pressures your colleagues or contacts are under in a new role.
✓ To understand the impact that changes in your client's industry might have on their business.
✓ To understand the impact of a key person leaving the business.
✓ To understand the shift in priority of their business.

The number one reason for questions is to

CLARIFY and DISCOVER.

Questions are like a bridge that connects knowns and unknowns, decisions and non-decisions and actions and non-actions. The questions asked are opportunities to ensure you're moving in the right direction with your client. It leads to answers that help you know if you need to act now, pivot, get rid of something, or solve something.

Once you understand *the purpose* of your questions you can then be more intentional with what you ask. You can walk away from the conversation with every piece of information needed, knowing what to do and what not to do.

Here is what you need to consider before asking your next questions to your clients.

Does this question help me solve, support, shape or sell something to my client?

- **Solve** a client's recognised need?
- **Support** a specific initiative already ongoing with your client?
- **Shape** or clarify a new project, offer additional insight or challenge?
- **Sell** or position additional services that may benefit my client that they haven't already purchased?

All of these questions are fine in their own right. But they should always be asked with the intent to deliver value and benefit to client.

Some examples

Solve – What were your thoughts on the development needs that came out of the last training session?

Support – How best can I support you in the change your department is facing?

Shape – How would you see us using our expertise to help you achieve that important goal for this year?

Sell – Had you considered what you'd do to ensure your data was fully secure?

As simple as these questions are, when you apply this framework of thinking to the planned conversations you have, you will become a master at asking questions. And you will be known as an insight-bringer and a person of value in your client's world.

Use the **questions worksheet** in your resources and decide on the answers you really need to know. Come up with 5-10 questions using this framework you could ask before scheduling that next call.

 # Summary of Step 2 - Set expectations

- Start the process of setting up your next client call with the view to get clarity of expectation of how you work together and your current relevance to their business.
- Decide what answers you need and prepare questions that allow your customer to draw out deep truths about not just the external symptom but the internal cause you can help solve.
- Use the questions guide and reflection sheet to help you develop more powerful questions.

Step 2

AMPLIFY TRUST

Trust is the foundation on which all relationships rest.

Trust is huge. There are a number of books out there that look at trust. I recently re-read Stephen M.R Covey's book *The Speed of Trust*. It suddenly hit me while reading that trust is on a continuum. It is never an event you arrive at.   This is something most people and businesses understand but few will have the patience for, especially when they're not seeing the growth or revenue they want. The levels of trust that truly generate massive results (beneficial to companies and their customers) take time and intentional effort to build. This is why amplifying trust is a pillar for customer success.

I explored the impact of trust in business through a survey I conducted of 200 customers through Qualtrics. I analyzed how customers perceived trust at different stages of their relationships with their suppliers and the *Client Trust Continuum™* was born. The Client Trust Continuum identifies **5 levels of trust** that determine where you are in your client relationship today, your ability to grow new opportunities, increase revenue and deepen your influence.

5 Levels of the Client Trust Continuum ™

L1 - Credible trust Demonstration of some value, showing an understanding of the client. Evidence you could solve a problem or help them get better.

L2 - Relational trust
Doing business together, delivering on what you've said. You now have more access to the client and regular communication.

L3 - Collaborative trust
Client comes to you with updates, needs and opportunities for your opinion, support or recommendation. You demonstrate good understanding of their business and creatively help them build a solution that helps them meet a goal.

L4 - Influential trust
Because of the first three, over time the reputation you build with your client allows you to get deeper into that business. You're given access to richer inside information about the client and further ways to help.

L5 - Intimate trust

At this level a client and the major stakeholders in the organisation trust you without question. They share their hopes, fears and concerns. You are part of their decision-making process (rather than just finding out the result).

Most sales professionals stay between L1 credible and L3 collaborative trust and they enjoy some level of success. What we should all be aiming for is L5. An independent 2015 survey from Qualtrics found less than 7% of businesses said they felt they had intimate trust with their suppliers. Most successful key account professionals get to L4 influential trust and those that get to L5 not only get 10X more than the average account manager but also see growth from their clients of more than 40% year-on-year.

Now you know these different levels of trust let's get tactical and explore three of the most powerful and underrated qualities you can nurture to develop trust. These three approaches if applied will move your customer conversations in a progressive and meaningful way so that you and your client benefit.

3 Powerful Characteristics of Trust Champions

Accountability

Do what you say when you say it. Be accountable for your actions. According to Covey's research in a 2002 Golin/Harris poll, "assuming personal responsibility and accountability" was ranked as the second highest factor in building trust. Great leaders and high-character professionals build trust by first holding themselves accountable then holding others accountable. Look to intentionally build on this area. Sometimes this means saying "no" and referring your clients to others who are best at that one thing. This a huge trust builder as you demonstrate high self-awareness and concern for your customer. Begin by identifying one activity you can share with your client every two weeks or every month that you can over deliver on. This could be making the commitment to share relevant articles or research connected to your client on a monthly basis. The more you over deliver the more reliable you're perceived as being and the more respect you gain because you've kept your word.

Consistency

Deliver results always. Simple, but one of the fastest ways to build trust and reputation is consistency. Fear and blocks to your sales can be removed when you are consistent. Consistency immediately amplifies your brand of reliability and puts you in a new category of the 'go to person'. This isn't always easy to deliver on as we don't work in isolation but with others. Remaining consistent isn't just about holding yourself to a standard but holding others and agreeing that so the entire customer experience is positive.

Empathy

One of the most recognisable traits of those with empathy is they are present and are deep listeners. President Teddy Roosevelt once said *"People don't care how much you know until they know how much you care"*. It's very true. Your ability to demonstrate empathy by being present, listening and showing understanding goes a long way. It can eliminate fear and get you to the *real reasons* behind the reason. This helps you to help others more and gives you unrivalled access and competitive advantage. There are numerous ways to nurture your ability to empathise. One is by practicing silence. Just being able to be still and listen will help you more intuitively to pick up on subtle emotional cues from your customers. You can demonstrate empathy through statements of understanding:

- "I can see how important this is to you."
- "I understand this can be frustrating."
- "I know this process can be confusing."
- "I'm sorry to see that you're in this situation."
- "I'd like to help you if I can."
- "Let's see if we can solve this together".

This obviously has to be done with sincerity but when said you can lower resistance and create a more open environment.

Summary of Step 2 - Amplifying Trust

- Check out the trust continuum info graphic. Print it out, put it on your desk and remind yourself of where you want to be in your client relationship
- Identify weekly tactics you can deliver on to help amplify trust using one of the three trust approaches or researching others you may feel more comfortable in.
- Make a note to re-read this chapter in a week to ensure it's fresh in your mind and you don't fall into complacency.

SKILL UPLOAD

ONE ADDITIONAL SKILL THAT WILL AID HOW YOU PREPARE FOR AMPLIFYING TRUST

Connect for Rapport

"With rapport everything is possible, without it nothing is possible."
Milton Erickson

Key account management is about understanding human interests and desires at a personal and organisational level. You should be constantly reading and building your skills in the area of connection and relationship building. The way we choose to think and the skills we choose to work on are the foundation to building success that is sustainable.

How are you intentionally building rapport?

Rapport has been put on the pedestal of social skills. No one can debate that people want to work with people they know, like and trust. This all begins with rapport or making a connection. How much you believe the above quote will determine how much influence and connection you gain with your customers.

There are so many ways we *'click'* and *'connect'* with others today. Let's get tactical. I want to share five proven ways to deepen rapport and connections with your clients. Using these approaches you'll be able to increase your relationship success today whether on the phone or in person.

Observe things that only someone close would pay attention to

I had a colleague named Matt who is a master at this. What people do, spend money on and talk about says something about what they value and do. If you can be someone who pays close attention to these things you're on the road to becoming a powerful connector. Matt had a client who was going on a trip she'd be looking forward to. It was in his home town New York. He not only mapped out an entire itinerary but gave them personal restaurant recommendations. End result the client had a great time and more business was booked because he took time to connect to something his client personally cared about.

Find common ground at every occasion and use this often

Take genuine interest in the other person and look for things you can agree on. If you have kids and they do too, that's awesome. Family is a huge emotive connector. Or maybe you notice the last few months your contact has taken weekend breaks and you enjoy travelling. Whatever that topic is, by sharing it, you raise your likeability. The key thing to connection and rapport here is to think mind-set. *"Powerful presence comes from being powerfully present"*. The more focused on the other person you are the deeper the rapport you'll build. The more connections you'll discover.

Be like them

We're all different: different personalities and behaviours. How we write emails, speak over the phone and respond to people in face-to-face situations are all expressions of who we are and how we respond to the world. Fortunately, despite all these differences, there are ways for us to make sense of the differences we have. I'd encourage you if you haven't, or if it has been a long time, to invest in a behavioural assessment tool. This is a tool which can give you greater insight into yours and others behaviour style. It tells you, how and why someone may react, relate to or show up differently in certain circumstances or with particular people.

What does this all have to do with connection? The better you understand your personality and behaviour and how it may impact others differently from you, the better enabled you are to adapt and connect with that person. To make a connection the three main ingredients are to be attentive, to be aware and to ask. Take note of the words they use and use them in your conversation. All these things add up to strong connections that can build significant rapport.

Give credit where it's due and show you care

We can often miss these simple words in business, *"Thank You"*. When you ask a client to share something or refer you and they've come through, take that moment to share that subtle, but relationship changing phrase. In fact I'd say you could go even further. If you notice something positive your client or their business has done, offer a sincere congratulations. Self-less actions are some of the most powerful demonstrations of connection. Something as simple as asking a client how the project went and if it went well. Self-less acts of others bring about commitment and trust in others. This is because it shows you care about what's happening with them and their business without it being about you. This can create a strong pull to reciprocate that gets your client to listen more openly to you. Eventually it leads to them trusting you with more opportunities.

Be positive

This may sound artificial and for some a no brainer! This isn't about excitement, energy or never being critical. But, rather it's a series of traits or characteristics you can learn to be someone more approachable and likeable. When I use the word positive it encapsulates smiling, being constructive, tone of voice, confidence, problem solving and much more. If you can cultivate a mind-set of positivity you'll approach every person and situation with a view that things will go right. Your choice of language and the way you treat others will be different. A great technique taught to me was called *'Hello old friend'*. The idea is to see each person you meet as an old friend you haven't seen in a very long time. Even in the most challenging of circumstances you can change your thoughts and inner chemistry to positively look at situations and find solutions. Another way to practice positivity is think about one thing you can do for a client each week that they haven't asked for. By force of doing this weekly you'll create a habit of positive action serving someone else. Being positive benefits you and everyone around you.

Note: If you're using the worksheet – have a look at the connection guide and write down one to five things you could do to connect with your customers this week.

<u>Step 3</u>

REDUCE RISK TO PURCHASE

Risk is your biggest challenge to explosive sales growth

"The biggest problems aren't always visible sometimes you have to dig deeper to find what lies beneath" – unknown

Arguably every sale we make has some element of risk to the person in front of us. Our job is to significantly reduce the perceived risk of purchase (of our service or product) to our customer. The reality is, even when we build trust with someone we still can't remove the primal nature of fear.

Whether we like it or not, self-interest drives most of our actions. Self-preservation is a strong and unruly thing that can sabotage, save and help you sell. Our clients' fear of risk is tied to their sense of self-preservation. As sales professionals we must understand this and work with this in mind. Eliminating risk to the client should be your top goal. Let's explore how you can become a master risk remover.

There are three primary risk drivers for clients that you need to know:

- Risk of personal gain/loss – What's in it for me?
- Risk of external perception – What will others say?
- Risk of future enjoyment - Will I regret it later? (not one people often consider)

During your customer conversations you need to be aware of these internal and external factors that drive decision making, regardless of what process you think they follow.

You need to help your customers

- Reduce the voice of internal risk and increase the confidence of external expectation with your product or service,
- Reduce the risk for your contact to his/her stakeholders, and

- Understand the risks and limits to your service that may affect future results.

The question is, "What perceived risks could your clients potentially have in purchasing your services today?"

The internal voice you may not hear is thinking
- ✓ I really can't afford this.
- ✓ I'll buy it another time.
- ✓ Not enough information.
- ✓ Not sure about the person.
- ✓ Not sure about the company.
- ✓ Not sure about the solution.
- ✓ Do we really need this right now?
- ✓ What will I really get back from this?
- ✓ What if I buy it and it doesn't work out?
- ✓ What will the boss think of this decision?
- ✓ I may be able to get it cheaper somewhere else.
- ✓ Our employees may not like it.
- ✓ My colleagues may disagree with my decision.

In all these scenarios the customer feels that the *risk* of purchase outweighs the *reward* of ownership. This is when you will hear *"I'll think about it"* or *"I need to talk it over with..."* It doesn't matter at what stage your relationship is.

If you're bringing something new, changing something old or simply asking for something different, the client's inner-risk voice will be active. This will be your biggest barrier to making the sale. Get mastery of eliminating risk through preparation and practice! If you eliminate risk, they will buy.

Steps to Prepare and Eliminate Risk in your Customer Conversations

Identify your risks to purchase. Some examples of this for you could be

- You are still not that known to parts of the business.
- You're in early stages of your relationship and still building trust.
- You haven't yet built a strong enough reputation with people they respect.
- You don't have other perceived resources or tools they might want or need today.
- They've tied themselves into a technology or process and yours may not be compatible.

You need to create great corresponding risk removers or reframes. Here are some ideas.

- Run a pilot, taster or sample of your product or solution, including other stakeholders.
- Create a joint proposal with the client that will be shared with the business and share the outcome.
- Identify specific customers in a similar position to them and facilitate a conversation between them. They act as an active example of that service.
- Invite other stakeholders to discuss ways they see your solution helping with the least amount of disruption.

Risk reframe statements and examples

- State that anything new will be slow, incremental and collaborative (prepare a clear pathway).
- If relevant, recall a time with the customer that a new project implementation went well. Agree with the client on the best aspects of that process and move things forwards.

- Review what the future big goal is for the customer and make the connection to your product/service specific and strategic to all stakeholders involved.

Do you recognise approaches you've used in your own conversations? If not take a moment and write them down.

 # Summary for Step 3 – Reducing Risk

- Decide to make intentional actions to reduce risk in every communication you have with your customers.
- Take note of your current conversations and what ways you can reduce risk.
- Outline 2-3 risk removers you can test in your customer conversations to move your sales forward
- Share your ideas with your colleagues and share successes.

Step 4

MAKE POWER CONNECTIONS

Why do more of the right relationships matter to rapid client growth? Think of strong client relationships as currency. The more of the right relationships you have the richer you become. It all depends on how you treat those relationships. One of the most challenging aspects of successful client growth is growing your internal influence, visibility and reputation within your client's business. This can be challenging for a number of reasons. Here are a few examples you may recognise and others you may not be aware of.

✓ Lack of wider business reputation means you have less access to the right people.
✓ Unable to provide the right level of value to warrant an introduction.
✓ Unable to determine who the right people are due to complexity of departments.
✓ Your company is part of a much larger network of suppliers solving a particular problem.
✓ You came in at the wrong level and now have to work harder for the referral up.
✓ Too early in the relationship.

Today's buying world is vastly different than in previous years. This has an impact on the relationship dynamic with our customers. It's no longer your contact who defines the relationship and purchase of your product or service but every stakeholder, influencer and sometimes end-user that has an experience of you and your business.

We all have varying experiences when it comes to growth with our existing customers. For the majority of key account managers and sales professionals we have to be patient. Make calls (that sometimes don't get responded to), manage multiple contact agendas, schedule meetings and much more to move to that next step in the relationship with our clients.

Your ability to identify, connect and build strategic relationships is one of the most important skills to cultivate in order to see massive key customer growth. It's why it is a vital component of the 4 pillars for customer growth success. All of this requires knowing more of the right people in and outside of your contacts circle of influence.

The questions to ask yourself are, "What ways are there to identify the right people?" and "How can I build meaningful and influential connections to increase my internal customer visibility, influence and ultimately growth?

Let's get tactical. I want to focus on four things you can do right now to discover high-value relationships within your client's business and connect successfully with them. This will require some effort but the rewards will far outweigh the work.

1. Get to know who's most important to your contact's world and why.

This is where you get to go beyond just understanding what's most important to your contact and begin to understand *who is* important to them. How do you do this? Simply be open, honest and ask. An example of this is,

"I'm keen to get to know more people in the business so I can really understand where and how we can offer the greatest value. When you think of key relationships I should be aware of in your business who comes to mind and why?" take notes.

You may need to build on this depending on how open your contact is and the context. If needed do a little research on LinkedIn beforehand and mention one or two names. Sometimes that by itself stirs more conversation and potential opportunity for referral.

2. Find ways to help your contact with those influential to them

Once you've identified some of those influencers, go back to your contact. Ask how you can help share information more easily with your client's contacts when working on projects together. Just listen and look for the best place for collaboration with your contact. Always assume ideas and proposals you share with your contact will be seen by other people. Now you know who they might be make your messages relevant, so that anyone in their business could understand how you help and how they benefit from it (think of it as inward content marketing).

3. Study the use trends of your product or service. What departments use it and benefit most from it? Who are the people involved in helping those employees on the ground?

For every service and product your client is using today there are people in your clients business talking about it (saying positive things, complaining or not really thinking about it all). That's just the reality. Being more aware of what is happening will put you in stronger position to expand your influence. Get feedback from the business. Ask if they'd be open to you asking a few select questions to managers. Once you've come to an agreement schedule those calls and prepare questions to gain insight that helps you better navigate your clients business and uncover more opportunities to help.

4. Get to know the managers of the end-users of your service/ product. Find the potential challenges they have, how you can help and who might lead that initiative.

Once you've had a few manager conversations, determine which managers support their employees and make decisions for their departments. Put together a list and create an email of what you discovered from your conversations including potential ways you could help. Share this with your main contact so they can also follow up on your behalf and benefit from being seen positively in the process. This is best so you maintain transparency. Be aware that depending on agreements you have with your client the view of this approach may be looked at differently. Take this approach as one you might need to test with only one manager first.

How to recognise connectors and influencers that matter

The reality is sometimes you'll speak with your contact and he/she won't know the people you need to know well enough. In some cases they may not even know who there are. Once you're in front of an influencer what do you ask to qualify whether you should really be investing time in them.

Sometimes they'll be kind enough to let you know, other times it won't be clear. Is there actually a way to identify the right people that isn't painfully time consuming? We're going to explore some of the most effective tactics for identifying the right people and making those power connections.

Before we jump in let's identify the four types of influencers and stakeholders you'll need to recognise and the roles they might play. At the highest level and complexity of buying decisions you'll find these four roles and potentially more.

Decision maker

Makes or approves the buying decision, can control majority of funding, often relies on others for information. Can sign or approve the contract or veto decisions of the selection team.

Potential interests and concerns

- Fits the budget; is affordable to own and maintain.

- Provides good return on investment.

- Achieves strategic goal.

- Builds competitive advantage.

- Heightens visibility or improves organisational image.

- Improves productivity, profitability and performance.

- Supports their personal reputation and stature.

How to recognise them

This is likely to be more than one person depending on the nature of your product/service and buyer profile. The decision maker will be the one responsible for bringing other stakeholders together, and making a decision based on potential options. This person may not be the decision maker every time. Your product or service may affect different parts of their business which may have different needs and processes. Here are two ways to identify other decision makers. **Let's get tactical.**

1.   Ask the question, *"What is most important to you in the purchasing decisions you make for your department or business?"* This uncovers priorities for decisions.

2.   *"How many are part of your team in making strategic decisions for your department or business?"* This question uncovers scope of authority.

Advisor

Assists or supports the decision maker, provides information and insight, highlights other organisational concerns or needs, assists in evaluating options and may recommend a solution or supplier.

Potential interests and concerns

- Offers insight and another perspective to the decision maker.

- Evaluates whether the proposal or company is the best option and purchase for the organisation.

- Will have an interest in the impact on the end user.

- Will be concerned about the impact and disruption on operations.

How to recognise them:

Advisors are the most challenging to find as they can be a range of different people based on the project's need. They often will know a wide range of people in the business but won't be a major decision maker. Let's get tactical.

Here are two questions to identify an advisor:

1. *"What is the impact on your role of decisions in your department?"* – This offers a side step question that gets them to share their position and will usually lead to naming other people more senior.

2. *"What information would you need right now and who else do we need to consider?"* – Again a side step question but gets you to identify the potential other players he/she may need to answer to.

Operator

Will use, manage, and, depending on the product/solution, consult with the decision maker. They will evaluate ease of implementation and impact on operations or performance. They may provide first-hand knowledge and experience and also recommend potential and preferred solutions.

Potential interests and concerns

• Does it make the job easier, faster, better or more cost effective?

• Is the solution compatible with existing systems?

• Is it easy to implement for me with the least impact on my team?

• Does it help us meet our goals and improve our capabilities?

How to recognise an operator

Operators are usually managers or heads of departments. Their opinion is respected and may have some say in the solution if they feel the delivery of this doesn't add value. **Let's get tactical.** Here are two things you can do to identify an influential operator:

1. Usually their title will give it away as it will be a functional manager role. This is not to be taken lightly as their role does not mean they won't have influence. Start with the question: *"What's most important to you about the impact of decisions made for your department?"*

2. Follow up with the question: *"What other people would this impact, and who might that involve?"*

Again another two stealth questions that gets them to uncover the influence of their position.

Champion

Not necessarily a decision maker but an important decision influencer. Sometimes the person is in plain sight and is the one initiating the change or project. The champion can help guide you to success. This person can help provide insight into individuals, issues and concerns. Facilitate access to key people and can alert you to externals who may influence the decision.

Potential interests and concerns

- Satisfies organisational needs solving the problem or supporting the goal.

- Presents them and the solution in the best light.

- Capitalises on their relationships.

- Product or solution is seen favourably in the business.

How to recognise a Champion

These stakeholders usually sit at a high level in the business. They may not be directly connected with your decision maker's department. Can be someone that oversees a department or region. They aren't concerned with the transactions and technicalities of what needs doing but rather the why, how and result. They can sometimes override or slow down decisions if they feel there is a better way. **Let's get tactical.**

Here are two things you can do to identify a Champion:

1.   Has an invested interest in the buying decision going well for them and their department. Will have delegated work but will still be notified of progress. Start with the question, *"What decisions are most important to make for you and your department this year?"* – Here we want to uncover priority and authority.

2.   Follow up with the question (as with the operator), *"What other people would this impact, and who might that involve?"*

Now you have a view of some of the major role players you need to be in connection with we need to get started on what I call the *Stakeholder map* TM.

Note: The Stakeholder map TM is a simple one page document that gives you immediate view of the influencers you've connected with, where they are, who they are what their connection is. You'll need this view as we move through the next steps.

 # Summary for Step 4 – Making Power Connections

- Make the steps and ask the questions with your contact to identify the right influencers in your client's business for your product or service.
- Use the profile statements to see if you can recognise other potential influencers and buyers in your client's business. Use the stakeholder map to log details about that person.
- Share your ideas with your colleagues and share successes.

SKILL UPLOAD

ONE ADDITIONAL SKILL THAT WILL AID HOW YOU PREPARE FOR MAKING POWER CONNECTIONS

Follow-up 2.0

Why add follow-up to this book? Because it's the most underused tool in your sales kit. As you connect with key people the way you follow-up will be critical. Frankly, I'm on a campaign to reinvigorate and revolutionise the follow-up process in client relationships. So let me ask you…have you ever said these phrases? Come on…be honest.

- Hi I'm just calling to follow-up…
- Hi, thought I'd catch up with you about…
- I was just touching base from our last conversation...

A number of sales people have these same old tired statements or surprisingly forget to follow-up at all. I was told early in my career, don't follow-up unless you've agreed to it already, there are commitments established or you have something truly of value to share. Anything outside of this and you become "human spam"… unrecognised, not of value and annoying. I can't point fingers here as I've been guilty of being all three, all in the name of *persistence*.

Why do so many sales people deliver such poor follow-up? I've noticed five main reasons many sales people fail at follow-up.

- They believe it's a numbers game.
- They call because they're hoping their client will buy something they haven't earned (tough one I know).
- They hadn't set clear actions on the last call and now have to back track to get commitment.
- They don't actually know where to take the conversation next (unprepared).
- They don't know what's important to the other person.

Harsh I know but if you really think about it, it's true for a lot of sales people. Maybe even you. Most sales people have no idea they have a pre- or post-sales follow-up process. Very few have a language to articulate it. We simply call it follow-up or, worse yet, account management.

You're told to stay close, build relationships and find more opportunities. Perhaps that may have got you this far. But to quote the great book by Marshall Goldsmith *"what got you here won't get you there"*.

I'd like to share a simple framework for thinking about how you turn your *follow-up* into a *value-up*. This can be used for new prospects but is mainly focused on taking spending clients on a journey where they benefit and, in the end, want to spend more money with you.

The main reason follow-up for many isn't effective is because it doesn't

- demonstrate any intention to deliver continual value,
- show the power of how your service/product is benefiting your client, or
- build on commitments for future purchase.

I'd like to introduce you to the new follow-up model or **value-up model. The ingredients to great follow-up need to be**

- **intentional** – specific and mutually agreed
- **valuable** – something that can benefit your client today
- **future focused** – helps to extend the conversation to a view of wider partnership
- **collaborative** – there is committed action for both parties to succeed

There it is. The raw ingredients for the most powerful follow-up conversations you'll have.

What could this conversation look like using this model?

Intentional
"Hi Bob, glad we've scheduled this call as I was thinking about our conversation. Although we're already working together I had some ideas I believe will significantly help you and your team.

Valuable

We thought about some of the key things that tend to slow progress with many of the clients we work with. We've built a video guide that will help you and the team more easily navigate and apply the system to your department. This will reduce the implementation schedule from 5 to 3 days, saving everyone 100s of hours and potentially 1000s of dollars.

Future Focused

We also want to ensure we're not tied to just this implementation. We also want to think about the growth of the company and what we might need to plan for later.

Collaborative

Would you agree, planning for this together would help? Great! Let's set a time to meet with you and the team so we can work out what role we'll play in making this happen".

Go ahead and give this process a go. Choose a client you need to connect and follow-up with and follow this process. It will change your approach, perspective and outcomes.

Step 5

CREATING VALUE THAT MATTERS

It's your responsibility to deliver value and insight. Value is one of the first concepts sales and business professionals hear about. *'Sell value not features!'* If we know all this, why do so many sales people and organisations struggle with getting this right? And why do so many clients complain they don't see it?

In this chapter we're going to look at how you can protect your value and create value that matters to your customers.

Your client's perceived value is a moving entity. Perceived value doesn't belong to you, but you can influence it. I saw this with my own clients when supporting a medium size manufacturing business in the UK. The client's use of our services and products changed over time, including the purchasing quantity. I explored this with these clients, asking some really specific questions:

- How relevant is our solution today based on when we started working together?
- How has the use and engagement of our solution changed for you in the last 12 months and why?
- What specifically have you and the business noticed about the change in use?

I was shocked at the wide variety of answers. The one element that remained consistent in their responses was that the same perceived value at the time of purchase had changed. The value we sold them at the beginning helped them at one phase of their business, but as their business pivoted, our service didn't.

They bought what they thought we had but not what we could really offer. *We just didn't see it.* This was a game-changing revelation for me as it pointed out that perceived value is not static but a moving entity.

> *Imagine this. You purchase a brand new IPhone from a provider. You're enjoying all the features and the service is great. Everything that you perceived you needed is there. An entire year goes by, your life and how you use mobile has changed dramatically. You now need to use different types of applications. You recognise your current phone doesn't offer what you need. Although you've had conversations with your phone provider you've seen no valuable updates despite seeing other competitors in the news. Renewal time comes and you get a call from your provider, asking you to renew your old phone or purchase a newer version of the same phone at a higher rate. Now, how excited would you be about that?*

Giving value is much like taking aim at a moving target. Only once we have a clear view can we take shot. All too often we take guesses only to come up empty. This may be the reason why some clients may not buy anything different or more of what they already have from you. Allow me to unpack this a little more with an example.

As simplistic an example as this is, clients today may be experiencing this from you or your company. Your customers are being asked to pay for the same service each year that hasn't caught up with what they need today. They may only buy again for ease, expectation and predictability.

As humans we love safety but self-interest is a much stronger driver. Eventually something kicks in which I've called *the Value Saturation Effect*. This is where the perceived value and effectiveness of your product/ service is viewed as less valuable over time when no improvements or advancements have been made. The impact of this is

- Loss of credibility with the client
- Potential loss of sales
- Loss of competitive advantage

How do you protect your value?

To prevent this saturation from happening you need to challenge the perceived value at different points in the life of your service or product: during purchase, integration, use and re-use.

Value perception gap with value infused

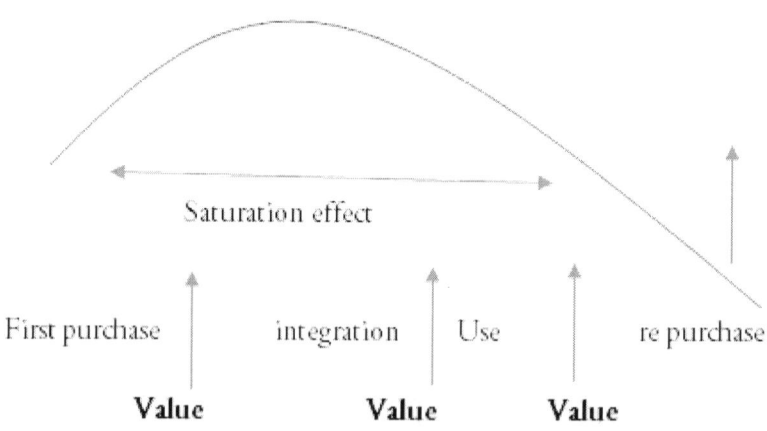

These are the times when the most support is needed. It is also when shifting client needs and priorities tend to happen: mergers, departmental changes, market disruption, contact leaves the business, etc.

You need to adjust your customer conversations to be sensitive to these inevitable shifting perceptions. Ask the right questions, speak to end- users and better understand where the challenges could be upfront. You'll be in a much stronger position to anticipate potential challenges and be more prepared to adjust when new information arises. This all helps to keep the perceived value of your product or service high.

No sales person wants a customer who simply sits on the status quo, even if it's your product or service. Eventually it leads to restlessness, and your clients ask, *"Why are we still using them?"*

The whole concept here is, what's important to your client today may not be the same tomorrow, three months or a year from now. Start taking note not only on what your product or service does, but also what your client and customers might need from you today, tomorrow, or a year from now.

How do we keep the perceived value of our product and service high? **Let's get tactical.** Here are three ideas that can transform your mind-set to delivering value for your customers.

1. Deliver great results that are consistently visible

You need to make sure you're delivering on and over expectations with your clients. Do it often and do it consistently. In step 8 I discuss how to deal with and build a great team. Collaborating and mobilising teams that deliver will be very important here.

2. Challenge assumptions and ask hard questions

Don't wait to know. Get to know so you actually know. Don't settle for client feedback with arbitrary forms and surveys. Get on the phone or get face-to- face with your customers. Ask great questions and listen as deeply as possible so you know the truth. Then take immediate action. I've spoken a lot about asking very specific questions. I'll continue on that theme. Knowing everything doesn't matter if you don't have a focus on the right things.

3. Help others in your client's business get the best from your product

Identify end-users and create a survey that puts them in the focus. Ask them to give feedback on challenges, value they see and observed results from using your product or solution. You may already have some great data. If so, what trends do you notice?

You'll want to use this data as fuel to influence your business and client to do something different. One important question to ask when you receive any client data, negative or positive is to ask, *"What is the potential impact of this information to my client?"* You can then discover potential ideas to suggest.

Action: Who in your clients business using your product or service could you get in touch with today to help?

How to create more value

One area I promote often with key account managers and businesses is to think more creatively about how they add value or, more importantly, create more of it. As you get to know your customers you have the competitive advantage to think for your customer and like your customer. They don't know your product or service better than you or the potential present and future benefits they could receive. You're client isn't siting around thinking about it. Here are three tactical things you can do this week to help you create more value.

1. Get to know the long and short term goals or priorities for your client and their business.

This will help you to schedule and prepare specific resources internally that you can share with your client periodically. Importantly find out what value would look like practically for them on a month-to-month basis. **An example:** If your client's aim as a business is for everyone to contribute to increasing their gross margins from 40% to 54% in the next 6 months then you can message and position your conversations in support of this. Share how your service or product could help them make that a reality. Your job is not just to promote what you're doing but maintain its relevance with where your client is.

2. Anticipate your short comings and gaps in service based on point one.

This is an important step. If you discover their goals and your solution does not provide the right technology, compatibility or relevancy for their business in the long term, you'll want to prepare to overcome that now. **An example:** Share the information you uncover with your manager and wider departments involved to find out how you can reduce this gap. Get creative and while you're working on this move to point 3.

3. Refocus and reinforce the value of the current work and impact your client is having today.

In the conversations you have weekly or fortnightly begin asking questions about observed differences after using your product or service. Speak about the future outcomes you're excited to see with them. You won't want to do this on every call. **An example:** Choose a metric that you've either agreed with your client or would normally use to measure successful implementation of your product or service. Send your client a short email with the great news. The more you can compound on the value that is noticeable the more value your client will perceive they're getting.

Note: All of these strategies do not take into account today's social world and the technology available to you. It's a fast paced ever moving beast. Use every relevant tool at your disposal to activate the benefits of these idea. You'll naturally come up with your own but the key is to take action.

 Summary of Step 5 – Creating Value that Matters

- Make the choice to create and not just add value this week.
- Observe the value your client says they are getting from you and explore how you can give 5-10X more.
- Share these ideas with your colleagues, friends and start creating more value for others.

Step 6

SHAPE FOR FUTURE COMMITMENT

You've found influencers and potential stakeholders or you've already been speaking with them. Now what?

That's the question asked by thousands of account and key account managers around the world. You finally find and connect with some of the right people in your client's business. Yes! How do you take those relationships forward? Or how do you turn them into bigger and better opportunities? If you read Step 4 you would've taken the initiative to make power connections and identify and connect with those influencers that matter. If not spend a little more time on that area as you'll need those people for this next phase.

I'm going to take you through a four stage process of direct tactics and approaches to discovering and creating opportunities with your contact and identified influencers. This will take some work but I've provided all the resources you need to make things happen.

The Stakeholder guide TM is the process by which you can simultaneously show your value and gain group agreement at all the right levels to move bigger, better decisions through the business faster.

Four stages that link the Stakeholder guide TM

Stage 1

Identify the one common thread that connects your contact and the stakeholders/influencers you've identified. Whether that connection is growth and profitability, retention of customers or savings on internal office purchases you need to discover it.

Here's how you can start. Get on the phone with your main contact and ask this one question, and listen very carefully. You're about to hear all you need to move into stage 2.

"What is the one goal or priority most important to you and the team to achieve this year and why?"

After hearing the answer if appropriate just say – Tell me more? And drill deeper to get as much depth and richness as possible.

The next question you might ask is, *"What would success look like for you and your department if you achieved that goal?"* Write down everything you learn and move to stage 2.

Stage 2

Verify what you've discovered by asking the same questions to other identified people.

Check with other contacts you have one-by-one. You could send a brief email like the one below stating what you've seen as an observation. I'd recommend speaking with them directly as well to ensure they're not simply agreeing because it looks vaguely right.

Example email

Hi Carol

I'm getting in touch because of a great conversation I had with (name of person). (Name person) and I spoke about the one priority that if achieved would set you and the business up for success in the coming year.

That one priority was (X) and I wondered what the potential impact of this might be on your department? I'd like to get your thoughts on this.
Even if your priority is the same or different this call will be really valuable. I'll be able to know the exact ways we can help you, the team and your department meet your goals this year.

What does your schedule look like next Monday at 4pm for a 10min call? I'll block the time and wait for your confirmation or an alternative that week.

Thanks

Stage 3

Collate the information and create an executive summary and high-level proposal

Here is where you would have collected the answers from your contact and those stakeholders. At this stage you may need to connect with your internal departments to manage your expectations of what is currently possible. Build that into the summary but also challenge what could be possible. Be open to the fact that you might need help. We talk more about collaboration and working with internal clients in step 8. I've shared an example of an executive summary below and in the resource page of this book with the stakeholder guide template. This will offer a great reference point to what you should look for.

Below are five points to remember when putting this executive summary together.

- It's all about them
- Show the benefit upfront
- Show a potential path
- Leave blanks for them to fill in
- Create strong call to action

Check out the executive summary below for reference.

STAKEHOLDER EXECUTIVE SUMMARY TEMPLATE GUIDE ™

Below are 5 points to remember when putting the executive summary together

It's all about them – Obvious but important to have front of mind

Show the benefit upfront – show the 1-3 things identified for each person

Show a potential path – What this means for each department

Leave blanks for them to fill – What's the missing opportunity

Call to action – What commitments are needed

Heading (example: Priority delivery high level report)

This report was prepared to help you and your departments achieve your priority goal.

Benefit

The one priority that connects each department in (name of client business) is (name of priority).

The impact, delivery and reflection of this for each department will be different.

The impact and benefit to (name of person) department is (XYZ)

The impact and benefit to (name of person) department is (XYZ)

The impact and benefit to (name of person) department is (XYZ)

Path

To get there we identified (X) elements to support success

Element 1

Element 2

Element 3

Missing opportunity

Elements 2-3 are not in place. Element 1 is but needs a clearer process to deliver more effectively. We'd like to get your perspective on where you see these working best or needing to be changed.

What next

After reviewing this I Imagine you'll have questions and perhaps answers to some of what we've proposed. Approaching each step one at a time we can measure progress, adjust for change and make continual progress to achieving success for every department. I'd suggest we set aside a more specific time to speak.

Stage 4

The last step is sharing the test proposal

Using the checklist I've provided as a guide we move towards the critical stage of sharing the proposal. The sequence in which you will do this is important as you want to get this right the first time. It can, and most probably will, take a while to get your contacts together.

The first thing to do is share this executive summary with your main contact and get them on board, framing this as a way to support and achieve a collective goal shared by everyone and meet a goal needed for the business. This is the chance to verify you've got the proposal right without fully committing.

You then need to share your idea of bringing these ideas to the group. Ask your contacts opinion on the best way to share this with his/her colleagues. If they don't have any immediate idea then you can suggest these two things.

1. Offer no more than a 30 min call with 15 min introduction and 15 min Q&A (make sure if needed you have the right people from your business or other on the call/meeting with you).

2. Ask for feedback and a commitment, *"Would you like to see a more built out map of what this might look like for you?"*

> *I worked with a key account manager named Sarah. She is an awesome account manager and seeing growth in her accounts year-on-year. Why would she come to me? Well, one of her accounts had gone through significant change. Seven of her business contacts had left within a year and she was struggling to find the right people and her opportunities were slowly drying up. She and the business were about to write-off almost 50% of the sales as something they may not recover from.*
>
> *I spent five days with Sarah looking at her accounts and one was slipping away. Taking a look at Sarah's client on LinkedIn we identified a few operators. We spoke with managers at different levels of the business and quickly identified an 'advisor'. Within three weeks we had 13 conversations with the business and found out the one priority they had and where Sarah could help most. Using the stakeholder email she brought those key people into a group call. At the end agreed an additional project worth 3x the amount of the projects Sarah had closed in the last 4 years. £1.2million. This all happened within the space of 8 weeks after Sarah had been in a slump for 6 months.*

Here is one example of the process in action.

We used the same executive summary stages, which you can find in the resource section. This could be your story. This isn't a fast process. On average this may take a 4-5 weeks. Once agreed you're on your way to step 7.

Note: Very few opportunities are unplanned, they're simply undiscovered by the sales person. Most of the opportunities are known to people your contact knows (we can't assume they're always told). The Stakeholder guide helps you discover those better opportunities. Some opportunities will require proactivity and insight before they become profitable. This is a great process to discover that.

Summary of Step 6 – Shape for future commitments

- Get to the worksheet and review the 4 stages to start your contact conversations.
- Check out the resources and example executive proposal before attempting your own.
- Share these ideas with your colleagues, friends and start creating more opportunities.

Step 7

CLIENT VALUE
MAP PROPOSAL

"Don't build it and wait. Build with them so your customers can buy" -
Anonymous

We're in an exciting place in the process to growing your customer sales. This wouldn't be complete without the natural process of proposing what you've discovered. I don't want you to just jump into this process. The Client Value Map or CVM is a way to consolidate the information you've gathered and present it in a more compelling way.

In principle you could use this same framework to enhance existing proposals and active opportunities you have.

This is not about a fixed methodology but rather one that meets you wherever you are in your customer conversation journey. The application of this is only fixed to your imagination.

You can see an example of what this could look like in the resource section of the book.

The structure of the Client Value Map has 8 sections:

1. **Present** - What you know about your client today
2. **Goal** - Where your client wants to be (outcome/results)
3. **Proposal** - Where you can help and the specific steps to implementation
4. **Expectation** - Their role in making things happen
5. **Future** - Future proofing against potential obstacles
6. **Value** - How you deliver even more value
7. **Build and Deliver** – Time it takes and what we do first
8. **Invest** – What we need to consider to take success past implementation

Putting this proposal together could take you a few days, maybe a week depending on the scope of work you're discussing. You'll notice in preparing this proposal that it will force you to think present, long term, and which ways you can provide value throughout the process.

This is critical because if your client can clearly see continual value they will be more open to opinion, more ready to change and higher pricing.

Sales growth isn't about selling new products it's about identifying value that achieves more for your client and your business. Sometimes it might just come in your product sometimes it won't.

An example of this process in action.

I worked with a Sales manager named James. His team was doing well but seemed to fall down at the proposal stage when closing. Initially he thought it was their writing style, thinking he should improve how the proposal reads and is seen and it becomes more compelling.

I introduced the Client Value Map (CVM) to James and we ran his team opportunities through the filter of the CVM. We quickly realised that the customer wasn't the focus, they weren't articulating the client needs very well, and they had missed out on huge opportunities to expand the value of the proposal significantly. We took the two most pressing proposals through the stages of CVM. The client was so impressed with how thoughtful it was they were asked to bid for a second opportunity and doubled the value of their proposal.

The Client Value Map is all the insight gathered from your client presented as the customer's story and you as their guide. You are positioning and personalising the process for them. All you need to do after is deliver then **review, renew and repeat**.

CLIENT VALUE MAP (CVM)

How to present a proposal that closes and generates more revenue immediately

1. Present	2. Goal	3. Propose	4. Expectation
What you know today about your client	*Where your client wants to be*	*Where you help and the specific steps to implementation*	*Their role in making things happen*
5. Future	**6. Value**	**7. Build and Deliver**	**8. Invest**
Future proofing against potential obstacles	*How you deliver even more value*	*Time it takes and what we do first*	*What we need to consider to take success past implementation*

Each step should build in clear commitments that support getting to yes faster, more easily and profitably. Each section should be no more than a page with highly personalised and specific content based on creating movement and actions for delivery. If you've identified all the right people in the 'Key Account Hack process' the 'Client value map' will only echo their exact words and discussions that will give you clear guidance on the places in that journey where you can see the investment that would need to be made. Each CVM done correctly can enlarge one single opportunity by 40% and even in an existing project add 10-20%.

CLIENT VALUE MAP (CVM)

How to present a proposal that closes and generates more revenue immediately

1. Present	2. Goal	3. Propose	4. Expectation
5. Future	**6. Value**	**7. Build and Deliver**	**8. Invest**

 # Summary of Step 7 – Client Value Map

- Review all the material you've collated and match content against the Client Value Map.
- Get to the worksheet and review the Client Value Map resource guide to start your proposal.
- Share these ideas with your colleagues and friends and start creating more value for others.

Step 8

GET THE RIGHT TEAM

Teamwork is the ability to harness the skills of two or more people collectively to a common purpose to achieve better and greater results faster.

If you're in a key account or customer managing role you are the personalised marketing channel for your company and the insight bringer for your customer. You connect everyone in your company to the client. Your collaboration ensures there is a clear view of what the expectations are when delivering value to your client. Your client gets the consistency of the customer experience and ultimately your customer growth success is protected.

How many of us in key account or customer managing roles intentionally build an effective team around our existing customers? **Why should you?** Other people slow you down and make your already challenging role more difficult. Isn't it simpler to do it all yourself? As much as I would like to believe that to be true it simply isn't.

To experience true explosive key account growth and deliver on that value consistently without a good team is nearly impossible. Let me be real. Just like me, you will have experienced success through your own graft, creativity, skill, planning and persistence. You should never lack in applying those skills and behaviours daily for your success and your customer's benefit. What we do need to do is refocus them for better and greater results.

According to research by CEB, documented in *Challenger Sale* 2011, in 91% of identified experiences of explosive KAM growth there was a direct correlation to high levels of team collaboration and distinct roles.

What does this mean for you?

It simply means when you push through on your own, you are potentially leaving money on the table. You could get bigger, better and more profitable growth with your customers by utilising an extra skill you've already been exercising but hadn't focused on.

Some of you may already have working teams and structures in place. Fantastic! Some of you may have people you can call on but no specific structure. Some of you may not have much at all or are unsure how to get the right people involved.

Whatever stage you're at the next section is for you. It offers a clear view on how to identify the right team, based on the accounts you're serving today and the resources and skillsets you might need to consider to get their involvement.

Identifying and building your team

The size and complexity of your account may determine the size and seniority of those people in the team that you'll need. Your team needs to reflect the identified people in your client's business. This will greatly add value to your customer and deepen the position and value of your company.

Here are four considerations to help you identify and build effective team alliances within your business.

1. Have some understanding of what your contacts might need that someone else in your business could add richer insight or value to. For example, if your contact is a financial director why not bring someone senior from your finance team to join you in a meeting who may better understand his/her issues. This immediately says you want to meet your client needs but also shows appreciation of the skills and expertise of your colleagues. You'll need them at some point.

2. Know your goals and use this to strategically guide your view of what you need to accomplish it. **An example**: Is your goal to renew a contract? Replace it with a more profitable one? Engage with the departments or managers that could help you meet that goal. Simple as that! Start the conversation. Work with your colleagues on the role you can each play to support one another and your client's for results.

3. View your business as if it were a client. Get clear on the common and strongest values that connect you, your customer and your colleagues from other departments. Identify your sales process and those specific stages where you're engaged

with your customer. Share this with your colleagues and agree to a structured way of working together that benefits them (their goals, wants, desires) and the client (service and value they deserve from you). Not an easy task, but powerful if connections are made. One way to start this off is to find one ally and work 1-2-1 through each department.

4. Set expectations for future collaboration with identified departments. Let them know that you may copy them into communication with the client. Do this from the perspective of leveraging their expertise. Clearly communicate their role and how important they are in it. All people want to be recognised and affirmed, so don't forget to say thanks.

Note: Don't always think the team needs to be in your own business. Sometimes in can be another client or someone else in your network. Sometimes you have to get creative. This won't happen overnight but the results of a team that works will far exceed the effort.

 ## Summary of Step 8 – Get the team

- Review the four ways to identifying and building your team. What one action could you take today to move that forward?
- This step is important. Choose to work on the skill of collaboration. Be different and intentionally go out to network across other departments and find mutual connections.
- Share these ideas with your colleagues, friends and start creating more value for others.

Key Account Hack System recap

We've explored a range of mindset shifting ideas and relational and tactical approaches you can take to get more from your existing client relationships.

My goal was always to make the process easy to follow and easier to implement with the resources made available to support you. More importantly, the entire process should be a natural part of your day-to-day client conversations in the real world.

This won't require you working another 10 hours a week to get it done. It will require focus and intentional daily implementation of these skills and approaches already discussed.

The Key Account Hack system is the structure in which you will use all the information you've learnt in this book. You'll have your own experience, skill and client history available to you to add together with all the new information you have gathered.

This system doesn't allow you to sit back and wait for orders to come in. If you follow this sequence like hundreds of other key account managers, you will have better and more meaningful client conversations. You'll know exactly how to work with key stakeholders and create bigger opportunities for you to help your customers more. All this for you means more revenue, more sales and you making more money.

KEY ACCOUNT HACK SYSTEM 8 STEP GUIDE

Deepening your client relationships and identifying massive sales growth

1. Set expectations *(Gain clarity for where are you now, what are your clients expectations and what have you agreed)*	**4. Make Power Connections** *(identification check list – using 'Stakeholder map' list those connections of major players and contacts)*	**7. Connect the insight** *(Using the Client Value Map or CVM document begin to work through eachstep using the client insight you've gathered)*
2. Amplify trust *(what tactics will you use to amplify trust to deepen your client relationships – List 2-3 decided from your worksheet)*	**5. Create Value that matters** *(how will you protect and create value– use ideas to choose 2-3 tactics you can apply)*	**8. Get the right Team** *(Ensure you have the resources and team to deliver for your client. List whatpeople, tools or resources mightyou need to get things done for your client)*
3. Reduce Risk *(what tactics will you use to reduce risk to purchase of your products and solutions - List 2-3 decided from your worksheet)*	**6. Shape the Future** *(You have the contacts. What small commitment can you get today to move the sale. Make note using the Stakeholder guide)*	

Note: You can find additional information on each section in the Key Account Hack book or reference resources

KEY ACCOUNT HACK SYSTEM 8 STEP GUIDE

Deepening your client relationships and identifying massive sales growth

1. Set expectations	**4. Make Power Connections**	**7. Connect the insight**
2. Amplify trust	**5. Create Value that matters**	**8. Get the right Team**
3. Reduce Risk	**6. Shape the Future**	

Time scales

This could all happen over a four week period depending on the resources you have available and amount of action you apply. This process is not about how fast you go through it. It's about the ability to do things skillfully and intentionally so at each phase you're funneling the information you need to help you and your client win. It's ok to be transparent about that in the process. This is ultimately about how your client wins in the process. If they feel they're winning, you'll win big too.

Note: If you're wondering where you put all the information you capture. I've created a one page worksheet for you to note down the answers, comments and discoveries at each stage of this process. You can use this editable worksheet provided to help guide conversations.

Wishing you all success in applying the thoughts and ideas curated here from combined research of over 200 customers and 100 highly successful key account professionals. I'm here to serve and help where I can.

If you have any questions about anything proposed in this book get connected at www.jermaineedwards.com **or email us at** support@keyaccounthack.com

All the best and look forward to hearing about your successes.

Jermaine Edwards
Founder of the Key Account Hack System

Resources

For immediate access to every resource in this book that you can access and print whenever you need it go to www.jermaineedwards.com/ivegotmybook

Resources you'll get access to:

- Client Value Map Guide
- Client Value Map Proposal
- Stake Holder map
- Stake Holder guide
- Reflection Questions
- Questions guide
- Trust Continuum Infographic
- Key Account Hack Recap
- Follow up guide
- Reduce risk sheet

Other ways I'd love to help you, your business or team

- Key Account growth Team Coaching
- 3-6 months Key Account Mastery programme
- Bullet 3x2 hour programs (Key Account Stakeholder influence, negotiating with procurement and executive conversations)
- Virtual communication webinar programme
- Key Client Growth Business Transformation

Also check out the great products at www.jermaineedwards.com

Resources I use and you can benefit from
- www.Kapta.com
- www.nimble.com

Links to website
Website: www.jermaineedwards.com
Twitter: @jsaedwards
LinkedIn: Jermaineedwards
YouTube: KeyAccountHack

To speak get in touch at: +44 (0) 203 701 5727
Or email us at support@keyaccounthack.com

Sign up and join 100s of account managers getting further advanced tips at www.jermaineedwards.com/signmeup

Did you enjoy the book?

I want to thank you for purchasing and reading this book. I really hope you got a lot out of it. I was just where you are in discovering the next step in my client relationships and sales. After interviewing over 150 super successful sales professionals. Surveying 200 customers. I now have a perspective and insight into customer relationship success that I've shared and many have now 3-5X more in sales in the first 6 months of implementing these skills.

Can I ask a quick favor though?

If you enjoyed this book I would really appreciate it if you could leave me a positive review on Amazon. I love getting feedback from my customers and reviews on Amazon really do make a difference. I read all my reviews and would really appreciate your thoughts.

Thanks so much.

Jermaine Edwards

www.jermaineedwards.com

The End

Author

Jermaine is an author, speaker and coach on a mission to help people reconnect with how they build effective profitable relationships with their customers. Father of 4, born in the UK, studied Economics in the UK and Germany.

10 years+ in large account management selling millions in services around the world. Speaking with 100s of account managers, directors and business owners sharing ideas to retain and see significant growth from their key customers.

Jermaine has breadth of experience that has allowed to him share success that is not only teachable but repeatable for anyone willing to think differently and take action. After surveying over 200 customers, interviewing over 150 successful sales professionals, key account managers, consultants and sales directors, he brings perspective and insight from multiple industries. You can feel confident the principles you learn will work and apply directly to you.

15548837R00046

Printed in Great Britain
by Amazon